SPIDERS

BY GAIL GIBBONS

Holiday House · New York

To Fred Lyon

Special thanks to Dr. Gordon Nielsen,
entomologist, Hinesburg, Vermont

Library of Congress Cataloging-in-Publication Data
Gibbons, Gail.
Spiders / written and illustrated by Gail Gibbons.
p.   cm.
Summary: Examines the physical characteristics, behavior,
habitats, and different kinds of spiders
ISBN 0-8234-1006-4
1. Spiders—Juvenile literature. [1. Spiders.] I. Title.
QL458.4.G53   1993   92-54414   CIP   AC
595.4'4—dc20
ISBN 0-8234-1081-1 (pbk)

Spiders may look scary but most of them don't hurt people. There are about 30 thousand different kinds of spiders.

Spiders come in many shapes and sizes. Some are so tiny that they are no bigger than a speck of dust.

Others can be as big as a dinner plate. Most spiders are brown, gray or black. Some have bright colors.

The first spiders lived about 300 million years ago, even before dinosaurs roamed the earth.

ARACHNID
(uh•RACK•nid)

Spiders belong to a group of animals called arachnids. The word arachnid comes from an old Greek legend. Once there was a woman named Arachne who was angry when she lost a weaving contest against the Goddess Athena. When Arachne died, Athena turned Arachne's body into a spider so she could weave forever.

A Spider's Body

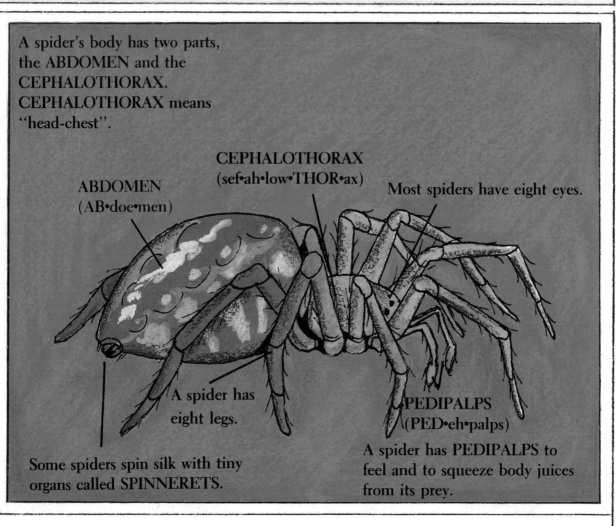

A spider's body has two parts, the ABDOMEN and the CEPHALOTHORAX. CEPHALOTHORAX means "head-chest".

ABDOMEN
(AB•doe•men)

CEPHALOTHORAX
(sef•ah•low•THOR•ax)

Most spiders have eight eyes.

A spider has eight legs.

PEDIPALPS
(PED•eh•palps)

A spider has PEDIPALPS to feel and to squeeze body juices from its prey.

Some spiders spin silk with tiny organs called SPINNERETS.

Spiders are not insects.

An Insect's Body

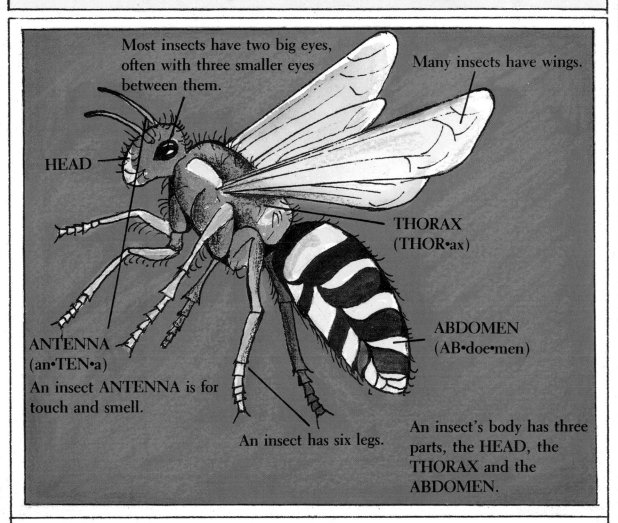

Most insects have two big eyes, often with three smaller eyes between them.

Many insects have wings.

HEAD

THORAX
(THOR•ax)

ANTENNA
(an•TEN•a)

An insect ANTENNA is for touch and smell.

ABDOMEN
(AB•doe•men)

An insect has six legs.

An insect's body has three parts, the HEAD, the THORAX and the ABDOMEN.

Their bodies are different from insects in many ways.

A male spider is smaller than a female spider. When a male spider finds a mate, he must be careful. If the female spider is hungry, she might eat him. Some male spiders do a dance or bring an insect to attract a female.

EGG SAC

SPIDERLING

A mother spider lays her eggs and encloses them in a strong, silk egg sac. Some spiders lay a few eggs. Others lay thousands. After a number of weeks, the baby spiders creep out of the silk sac. Spider babies are called spiderlings.

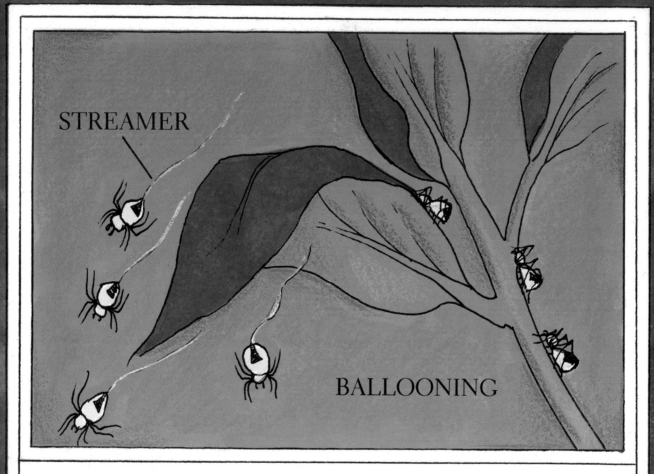

STREAMER

BALLOONING

Most spider mothers don't stay with their babies. Some spiderlings care for themselves as soon as they are born. They run up to the highest places they can find. The spiderlings spin out long streamers of silk. A breeze lifts them and carries them to their new homes. This way of travel is called ballooning.

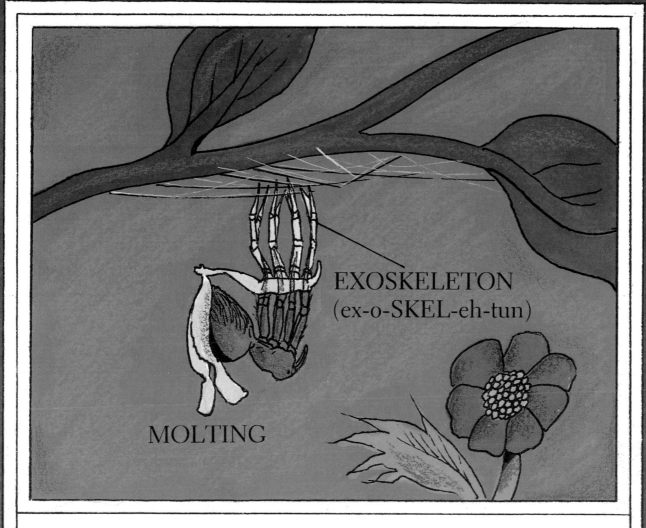

EXOSKELETON
(ex-o-SKEL-eh-tun)

MOLTING

As a spiderling grows, its hard outer skin, called an exo-skeleton, becomes tight. The skin cracks open along its back. The spider sheds it by climbing out. This is called molting. Most spiders molt five to ten times.

TANGLED WEB

HOUSE SPIDER

Some spiders are web weavers. They spin webs to catch their food. There are spiders that weave tangled webs. The spider spins a tangled mass of silk. When an insect is trapped, the spider runs out to get it.

CARDINAL SPIDER

SHEET WEB

Other spiders weave sheet webs. The spider hangs upside down beneath the web. When an insect hits the sheet web, the spider quickly pulls it through the webbing.

FUNNEL WEB

GRASS SPIDER

Spiders create funnel webs, too. The top is big and the bottom is small. The web is held in place by lines of silk. The spider sits at the bottom and waits for an insect to fly or walk in.

TRIANGLE SPIDER

TRIANGLE WEB

Some spiders spin triangle webs. A triangle web is fastened at three points. The web's bands of dry and sticky silk trap insects.

First, the spider spins a few lines of silk to hold up the web.

Then, it adds lines of silk that look like the spokes of a wheel.

Around and around the spider goes, adding a sticky coil to the spokes.

Next, the spider waits for its meal in the center of the web, or it waits nearby.

The orb-weaving spider spins a pattern of many circles.

When an insect lands on the web, the web shakes.

Instantly, the spider pounces! It wraps the insect in silk. Then, it stuns the insect with its poisonous fangs.

ORB WEB

GARDEN SPIDER

If the spider is hungry, it eats the insect right away. If not, it waits until later.

The most beautiful spider web of all is the orb web.

WOLF SPIDER

Not all spiders use webs for catching food. Some hide in burrows or beneath rocks and stones. When the spider sees an insect, it quickly runs out and grabs it.

WATER SPIDER

One unusual kind of spider lives under water. It weaves a bell-shaped web. Then it fills the web with tiny bubbles. The spider stays there, breathing the air from the bubbles, and waits to catch water insects.

TRAPDOOR SPIDER

Another type of spider digs a tunnel and lines it with silk. To protect itself, it makes a hinged trapdoor from dirt and silk to cover the tunnel. When the spider is hungry, it opens the door a bit. If an insect comes close, the spider scurries out to catch it.

CRAB SPIDER

Some spiders hide on or inside flowers. One spider even changes color, from yellow to white, to match the color of the flower. When an insect lands, the spider snatches it.

BLACK WIDOW SPIDER

Some spiders are dangerous. One of them is the black widow spider. The black widow spider bites only when its web is disturbed or it is in danger. The poison of a black widow spider can kill a person.

TARANTULA

The biggest spider of all is the tarantula. When its legs are stretched out, it can measure about ten inches wide. It is very hairy. Tarantulas that live in the United States are not poisonous to people.

Spiders have enemies. Some insects, like spider wasps, hunt and eat spiders. Toads, frogs and some birds like to eat spiders, too.

Most spiders live for about one year. Some live much longer. Female tarantulas sometimes live to be 25 years old.

Many people don't like spiders because they are afraid of them. But spiders help us. They play an important role by eating many insects that are harmful to crops and people.

Spiders can be interesting to watch. Scientists are still discovering new kinds of spiders and learning more about them.

Spiders...spiders...spiders!

 Remember the nursery rhyme, "Little Miss Muffet"? Little Miss Muffet was a real little girl. Her father was a spider expert who used to make her eat mashed spiders when she was sick. About 200 years ago, this was a common cold remedy.

Some spiders can walk on water. The raft spider does this by spreading its legs wide while it takes quick steps.

 Spiders have an excellent sense of touch. Their bodies, mouths and legs are covered with fine sensory hairs.

 EEK! A person who is terrified of spiders has arachnephobia (uh•rack•ni•FOE•bee•uh).

 Spider silk is three times stronger than steel thread the same thickness.

 The deadliest spider in the world is the Brazilian wandering spider.

 Spiders don't stick to their own webs because their feet are specially shaped and their bodies are covered with oil.

Some spiders spin a special line called a dragline. If an enemy comes, the spider can quickly drop down the dragline and escape.

  Not many animals eat ants because they taste badly. One spider is protected because it looks like an ant. It is called an ant mimic.

 Spiders can walk up walls and across ceilings, because they have special grip pads on their feet.